AMBUSCADE

poems by

Brian Ascalon Roley

Finishing Line Press
Georgetown, Kentucky

AMBUSCADE

For Gwen, Aidan, Brendan, Tom & Azucena

Copyright © 2021 by Brian Ascalon Roley
ISBN 978-1-64662-412-6 First Edition
All rights reserved under International and Pan-American Copyright Conventions. No part of this book may be reproduced in any manner whatsoever without written permission from the publisher, except in the case of brief quotations embodied in critical articles and reviews.

ACKNOWLEDGMENTS

Thanks to the editors of journals and anthologies who published poems that appear here or will appear in a later book but whose feedback taught me to write these: *Fence, The Iowa Review, Columbia Poetry Review, Intima: A Journal of Narrative Medicine, Presence, the Maine Review, the Asian American Literary Review, Kuwento For Lost Things* (Carayan Press).

Publisher: Leah Huete de Maines
Editor: Christen Kincaid
Cover Art and Design: Carla Roley
Author Photo: Carla Roley

Order online: www.finishinglinepress.com
also available on amazon.com

Author inquiries and mail orders:
Finishing Line Press
PO Box 1626
Georgetown, Kentucky 40324
USA

Table of Contents

PART ONE
Ambuscade 1
Aswangs of Los Angeles 2
Kanlungan ["Tsissmis"] 6
Bukas 8

PART TWO
Adopt a Daughter 9
Sibling Rivalry 11
School Bus Father 13
Iron Curtain ["Elderly Children"] 14
Organ Exchange 16
Holding Court 17

PART THREE
BITTER CHERUB
I.
The Aswang Of Pacific Heights 20
Shriveling Meal 22
Notice 23
Stay At Home Dad 25
Bedtime 27
The Husband, In Late Childhood 28

II.
Caregiving 30
Elderly Lady 32
The Rooster 33

PART ONE

AMBUSCADE
1901

How could you see a man (let alone capture him) in civilian clothes, who kept his bolo knife and rifle in the bushes, who waved your country's flag at you with smiling faces and shouted the word "amigo" until you passed, then cut you from behind? What does it do to your psyche to live like that?

You came perhaps from the arid plains of Kansas, East Texas, Nebraska; you learned to use a rifle hunting antelope, sighting them from cover of bouldered outcroppings on open plains; you learned to track deer and wolf from your father and grandfather over barren landscapes; you knew how to track the last Comanche by looking for rare springs of water, the defensible outcropping, the lone tree shade.

But now the very air was water, so hot your clothes clung to you, and vines in your face slowed you down. Insects woke you at night, crawling on your face, and unfamiliar snakes coiled in your belongings, scorpions burrowed in the boots you reached for on waking from your troubled dreams

of the sudden ambuscade, of small patrol units in the jungle, of unreadable smiling faces, of a rebel general possessed with anting-anting—mystical powers said to resist your bullets
and capture

and you began to dream their words, in your slumber, their mysterious music at first,
at once Malay and Iberian, and then starting to understand them, to believe their music, to know

you are the hunted.

ASWANGS OF LOS ANGELES
1994

1

Sometimes on hot glass-rattle nights
of the Southern California desert winds
which roar through our city
and irritate our windows and dreams
I will dream about the aswang.

I grew up on stories of these Philippine
ghost vampire witches
who look human during the day
but at night sprout wings and detach
from their lower bodies and take
to the skies.

They leave their legs behind and fly
about with their entrails dangling in search
of victims they had identified
during the day. They seek out pregnant
women or people whom they feel
have slighted them. (You might
have stolen from one in business
dealings, thinking her human; bumped
into her impolitely at market;
or simply looked at her the wrong
way).

It will land on your house
or nipa hut roof
then crawl over thatch looking for the place
just above your bed.

They especially like pregnant women. They will dig
a little hole
over your sleeping body
then lower their long tongue
above your slack-open mouth.
They drip a special evil saliva
into the mouth
and it brings back up the blood of the victim or, if she is pregnant
the blood of the fetus.

*

The mother wakes up the next
morning with a dead baby inside her
shriveled up, a strange feeling
within.
Sometimes the woman, not knowing
where this feeling comes from, wanders about in search of something
she does not understand.

Some hang themselves, take poison, drown themselves in waves.

2

In the region of my clan adults shut their shutters at dusk
because they do believe
in the aswang.
Because they were educated
by Belgian and American nuns
in U.S. colonial Manila, my mother and tita
did not do this, having been admonished
not to follow
such native superstitions. But the yayas snuck into our room
after bedtime
and shut the shutters
to the night.

*

Even in Santa Monica
my lola would tell my sister and I
to watch out for the aswang
and we would say "But
we are in California"
to which she replied "That does not
matter. They follow the Filipina wherever she
may live in great numbers. Everywhere,
to Vancouver, Saudi, Kuwait, Los Angeles,
New York, Bermuda, Madrid.
It does not matter if people do not notice
us in our great

numbers. The aswang does. She knows. She can smell
our tsissmis, the excitement of our scandals
the vibrations of our
laughs."

"You are saying they cross the Pacific
Ocean just to find us?" Sister asked.

"Oh yes." Lola clucked her tongue and made a nod.

"That's impossible."

"Hoy, she rides on a ship, sleeping in the dark cargo
bays during the day."

"But why?"

"Remember, it is easily
offended."

3

Even now
on hot nights of the desert winds
which are said to irritate
Los Angelenos but make Inay turn on all the lights
of her house and run the vacuum
loudly
I shut my eyelids and can see them
descending on the paper rooftops
of Venice Beach, California
their winged half-bodies taking
care to avoid the power lines
which will entangle their delicate
spans.

KANLUNGAN ["TSISSMIS"]

Alone, at home, I went to bed.
I did not shower because I wanted
to keep the smell of her skin
and memory of its sea-taste
with me. The wind was strong
and creaking.

The whole house
swayed and I drifted
off to sleep. I dreamed
of the bitter manananggal

I'd told her about.
She laughed in my arms as if
at some fairy tale
and I said, No
pressed my finger to her lips, stroked
her head against my chest because I wanted
her to stop, listen

to those winged half-torsos
the creeping fingernails on rooftops.
Night became warm
my boyhood country, the warm dropped mangoes outside
smelling up the humid garden
air. My boyhood bed musty and
my mind filled with the noise
of cockroaches scampering
like sand beneath.

Bats outside.
Creatures the size of monkeys, landing
on treetops and creeping
among branches.
The floating voices of maids and titas laughing
over tsissmis
at somebody else's expense.

The shutters bolted by iron
because the yayas knew.

"Why?" she asked, cheek against
my chest, trying to listen for organs.

"It's bad luck to talk about them."

"But I thought your grandmother talked about
them all the time?"

I scratched my chin. "We couldn't help it."

BUKAS

I was asleep but aware that my mouth
was open. I heard the sound
of the creature landing
upon my rooftop, crawling about, digging
a hole
in the shingles with its long fingernails. It let down its long tongue
the evil saliva entered my mouth. I was a woman now, had a womb
and fetus in my body. I felt the fetus
begin to shrivel up inside me. I tried to scream
but no words came out of my mouth.

PART TWO

ADOPT A DAUGHTER

My ovaries are too old
and shriveled
up, my wife said
and besides, I am tired.

Then let's adopt a girl, I said,
girls are better caretakers anyway. If she was two, or three, she'd be
easier to get
than a baby.

She said: I don't think I could give up our own blood
children's financial resources.
Emerson is going to cost a lot; he might need personal
assistance after we die.

That's why we need to adopt a daughter, I said.
Right now he only has a brother. You never know how a brother
will go. Two siblings makes it more likely one of them
will stand up to the plate and take care of him
when we die.
And especially a girl, I said: You don't teach these college
boys like I do.

Where are we going to get her? We don't make enough money.
They won't let us adopt one, especially since we're so old.

Maybe we can get one from the Philippines; she could teach
the boys Tagalog by talking to me
if she's old enough. There's too many people
there anyway.

My wife shook her head.
Think about what you are saying. What about the girl?
Do you think it would be fair on her? Do you think
you could love her just as much too?

I walked to our son's bedroom door and watched him
napping. His mouth agape, head limp to one side.
You try to think of such a child as normal
as capable as anyone else
because you are supposed to and because you do not
want to hold him back; but also because it is easy enough
to deny his difference
and the future, when he laughs.
But when he is sleeping you can see his slack face
and recall last night when he vomited
and you took him to the hospital for an IV
drip, had to help the nurse
hold down his arms, while he struggled
and screamed
and the gurney bumped as a second nurse
maneuvered to push the needle into a vein. And I did it
held him down
kissed his ear sweetly
while his legs kicked my chest and he screamed
No, daddy! Please!
Gathered courage by the possibility of his pale
bluish face there on that hospital gurney
his lips turning cold
and mute.

SIBLING RIVALRY
Voice of Isabel

Your little boy brain cannot
understand why we smile at him
more than at you.
Perhaps someday you may appreciate
what it is like to have a doctor
tell you that your child will die
young, if you lack vigilance.
How a cold afternoon can encumber
an already overburdened mind.
How a simple cold can fell
him. But at what cost to you, Diego?

Lately you have been hitting
him in his walker, or wheelchair, tipping
it over from the back. He fell face
forward the other morning, cheek against
the dirt, knocking a tooth out,
pinkish and bloody. You stole his beloved
stuffed cat, gouged her eyes with my
purple grading pencil. Returned Kitty
onto his bedsheet, ready to be found
with cloth worming out of her sockets.

You have discovered his emotional lability
that frontal lobe damage that can
make a person cry simply by seeing
a cartoon character frown
or to laugh in response to a stranger's
smile. You have learned, by now,
how to make him weep
by presenting a sad face, by killing a butterfly
against the glass, by telling him Mommy
was sad last night because
he cannot walk.

They say we are not supposed
to over-mediate in sibling fights.
Perhaps I do overreact
when I come over to break it up
my voice frightening your eyes
my feet pounding wood floors
demanding, What have you done, Diego
to make your brother so upset?
You look down, frown, face
in an angry sulk. You say, Nothing
but look up to see if you had pushed
too hard.

I see the fear there, stop myself
from grabbing your hand
to drag you to time out chair. Instead,
I gather my breath
kneel beside you
direct your face to mine and say,
Do you know you are your brother's keeper?
You are four, he is seven
and already I am anticipating
my own death.

SCHOOL BUS FATHER

We read about the father who stepped onto
his daughter's school bus to confront
the other children, after he learned
they had thrown a condom

at her hair which became sticky. The daughter
had cerebral palsy and suffered difficulty
getting it out with her spastic
fingers and was laughed at
and had been laughed at for weeks

and this father shouted at
the boy who did this
told him if he humiliated
his daughter again he would fuck

him up. And he turned to the other kids on the bus
and told them he knew they had laughed
and if they laughed at her again
he would fuck them up

 too. It turned out that the condom had actually been thrown
at another disabled kid and now an investigation
was being conducted against this father by disapproving
school authorities. But what interests me is that

TV reporters speaking about this father
made little laughs, on camera, as if embarrassed
for the man
and felt a need to say, What he did was inappropriate—of course—but
man, his girl did have cerebral palsy.

IRON CURTAIN ["Elderly Children"]
Voice of Isabel

Why do our children resemble old people
as they walk with tiny colored canes,
hunch over their soggy paper plates,
try to sit upright without losing
balance, lift forks to their mouths
with trembling hands, lean
on tables and railings as the morning draws
on and their faces begin to sag
eyes grow spacey
double chins rest against
their little chests?

The doctor tells us we are all
in a way afflicted
our mitochondria degrading over the years
dwindling our bodies and brains down
to the withered state of being
we will reach if we are lucky enough
to live long enough to be considered
elderly. Her voice is accompanied
by consoling eyes, which is perhaps what passes
for bedside manner as taught in medical schools
these days.

The Hungarian conductors
trained in orphanages using strict
techniques developed during a time
of occupation
on spastic children taken from their parents,
seem wiser in bedside manner
much blunter
though it is hard to know
how much of that could be due to accents.

They say there is no point in asking why
god decays the bodies
he gave us, a waste of time to try
we need to get on with it.
We are not to decide for them, or try to change
them, as if they need fixing. We are not
to help them, baby them, hold them,
lift them up when they twitch in pain
as they try to stand
or they will fail to achieve
independence from their parents
as other children do.

The head conductor tells us not to feel pity
for them simply because they do not
meet other children's milestones, or walk for after
all they do experience joy

as if joy is all that matters
and perhaps that is something to chew
on, though I suspect she tells us this
not for the children or the truth
but for parents.

ORGAN EXCHANGE

You read about the fathers
who give up an organ
or body part for their sick
suffering kid. On TV a man wanted
to give his heart to his boy
who had the ragged-red fibers heart
disease we knew about
but the doctors wouldn't let him
so he hung himself.

But unfortunately or fortunately
depending on your perspective
he didn't quite die, didn't quite
finish the job, so he begged the maverick
doctor who breaks all the rules
to give the boy his heart. I'm about to die
anyway.

But it doesn't work
that way, the doctor said. The heart
goes to someone
in a queue.

Then I wouldn't give it out
to anyone.
You have to do it
please
he begged.

I would do it, the doctor said
but you damaged
the heart.

HOLDING COURT

"Wheelchair boy" some kid said
as we entered the hotel lobby.
Later, another one asked me,
"What happened to him?" as I helped
you walk to the bathroom
by holding your hot, six-year-old hands.

Later that night, in the restaurant bathroom
a third boy asked, "Why are you in that?"
and I forced myself to let you answer
for yourself and washed my jittery hands.
"I can't walk," you said, so I took
your hands, helped you wobble
to the sink, then placed your palms
beneath the water and soaped them
whispering, "You CAN walk.
You just need a walker or hand to help."
You answered, apologetically,
"I just meant I can't do it on my own"
and lowered your eyes.

The apologetic tone hurt me like
an uppercut and I swore at myself
not to show my worry
and kept a tight smile as children
came up to us in the pool singing
that cheerful phrase "the wheel chair boy."

At night, our puckered skin smelling of chlorine and sea in bed,
your mother and I wondered what the other
kids say to you at hotel *day campo.*

Back in snowy Ohio, we saw you in your classroom
trying to talk in your halted manner, and other kids would give up
listening before you finished
and just walk away.

The *campo* is really just a prettified day care center
done up in fake Tahiti
with eucalyptus spa scents meant to cover
up the smell of disinfectant and potty,
where bamboo-framed windows open
to the breezeway so that adults
can peer in as they pass and make sure staff
are not abusing children.

My mother passed by, her necklace of wilted
airport orchids still dangling about her neck,
glanced in and saw
you there, at the head
of the table, talking, as other kids watched on.

"He was holding court" she told me later
and giggled with her Filipina cheer
to which I said "What do you mean, 'Holding Court?'"
"I mean they were watching him talk."
"Who?"
"The teachers. Other children."
I shut my eyes and tried to imagine this.
The rumble of the sea on sand felt different
here in the middle of the Pacific Ocean
than in the cradle of my late childhood, the coast of California.

"Did they seem interested or entertained?"
my wife asked abruptly, looking up
from her magazine and leaned
forward with hunger.

My mother seemed confused
and searched her memory
to discern the meaning. She often mistook meanings
due to the slipperiness of accents.
"What does it matter?" Mami
said: "They had his attention."

I leaned forward, licked my lips,
and said,
"Tell me more."

PART THREE

BITTER CHERUB

I.

THE ASWANG OF PACIFIC HEIGHTS

The first child was lost
sometime in Pacific Heights
though they did not know
it until the doctor woman
put the ultrasound to the mother's belly
to look for a beating heart

but grew grim-faced
and tried not to frown though they knew
she'd found
                       silence.

Why did it happen? the mother
asked; and the doctor shrugged
and said
Have you ever miscarried
before?
The mother touched her cheek. No. Well, once.
I found it in a toilet.
She looked at her husband and then back
at the doctor woman.
It was from before, you know
when I was young.

Later, that night,
the mother told her husband
about that hollow feeling of terrible emptiness
and air inside
as he placed his arm around her shoulders
and tried
to feel
the same.

SHRIVELING MEAL

The aswang must have come to visit them
again, some anonymous
night, landing on the rooftop
of their building
in Pacific Heights
poked its fingernails through the red roof tiles
above the master bed
and let down the long tongue
and dripped
the special saliva
into
her open mouth
        to bring up the blood
                of the fetus.

Yet this time, it did not finish
did not complete the shriveling meal.
Was it scared off? Had it heard
some animal sound, or ambulance
scream from the hospital nearby
and fled
having only taken
away a part of the baby—
a snippet of foot
perhaps
or spinal cord
or neuron
before it abandoned its project
leaving baby diminished
yet still alive
and fled
north beyond Tiburon?

NOTICE

Come morning, the mother awoke, smiled
unknowing
at the lace curtains laced with sun.

They would not even notice
for years
what was missing
in the beautiful boy

would not
(how could they not?) even
             notice the way he slumped back in his stroller
the tired bags beneath his smiling eyes
the slow way he played with toys
on the floor
or at Alta Park
on sand.

Then, suddenly
inexplicably
on a certain day
at that park in Pacific Heights
where you can see out
on a hillside of oft-photographed Victorian rooftops
she found herself looking down
watching his pudgy wrists
—oh! she suddenly frowned, looked up
at her husband and said: he seems very floppy here,
on the sand.

Don't you worry, he said.
You worry too much.

But the other kids don't just sit there like that
and, Amado, oh my god
the way he slouches in his stroller
on our walks!
It's not normal. You're the one at home with him.
You haven't noticed that?

No. He blushed, stiffened. He watched the boy, fifteen months old, crawling
about on the sand. You're freaking out, honey
over nothing, he said softly.
They say that kids develop at different rates.

You think I'm being silly? she asked
touched at her hair uncertainly.

Yes.

She smiled and looked down
at their baby—a toddler now
who could not yet toddle—
and brushed sand from his hair and gave him
a kiss.

Of course, she laughed, twirling her hair with embarrassment. It's a sin not to feel
grateful—not to realize
we're blessed.

STAY AT HOME DAD

But the husband now, who "stayed at home
with the baby"
began to notice his son's slouch (in car seat and stroller)
and a flat place at the back of his head
still soft
where he slept.

Doctor, it's flat, he said.
The doctor man gave them a helmet
for the boy to wear
with bright boy colors
(on which the mother placed car and truck stickers)
and the father felt remorse at how he could not
have noticed before

and passersby stared at the boy's helmet
and the father smiled at them brightly
even at women who frowned
judgmentally at him
for what he did not

know. He did not know
many things, but they took
the boy to a neurologist
(that repository of knowledge)
and she looked at the boy in the waiting
room try to stand up holding the
aquarium leg

smiling at the fish
(ankles wobbling)
and she said, Does he always
stand like that?
They hesitated and looked at each
other. Well, yes.
She made a mark in her pad and walked
back into her florescent hall.

They waited. Half an hour later a nurse came out
and asked for their address and wrote
it on a pad of paper. She looked about
to leave.

Nurse, the mother ventured, with a timid
voice. When is the doctor coming back out?

The nurse kept her eyes on the pad
a moment, then looked up at
them. Out? She's not.

The mother gripped the husband's
hand. He stepped forward and said,

But we assumed she was going to tell us;
she just walked off and we assumed.

We'll write up a report and send
it to you, replied the nurse. The mother said,
But did she tell you anything?
Does this mean he's all right?

The nurse looked over at the boy
who crawled at the legs of the fish tank
smiling up at the glass
giggling happily
which suddenly sounded to the man
like the cheerfulness of somebody
you thought of as retarded.

Please, he said.
The nurse glanced back at the receptionist window
empty now
and then eased close to them and whispered,
Dr Kaiser said she wants to do some tests. She said that,
well, she thinks they'll find something wrong
with him.

BEDTIME

He found the mother on the toilet
that night, just sitting there
after putting the boy to bed.
But he didn't do anything wrong. She shook her head.
I just don't know what I did wrong.
I just do not get it.

You didn't do anything wrong, he said.
We must have done something, she said,
something I ate, or maybe I shouldn't have worked
so late
or stressed out so much
I knew I shouldn't have taken a flu shot
(she looked into the mirror: mouthed: you bitch).

It's not a flu shot. They wouldn't let you take it
if it could do that
to a child.
She looked up at him harshly.
But there's nothing He did wrong, she said. You can't deny that.

Come to bed, he said and held out his hand.
She looked at it, shook her head
and stared forward at the bathroom wall
on the same toilet in which
she had once found a fetus

shriveled up, floating, curled forward
as if trying to kiss
       its knees
              for comfort.

THE HUSBAND, IN LATE CHILDHOOD

1

it's just stories they made up
to frighten children
the sister said

oh no, Lola clicked her tongue
and shook
her head. It was not for the children
that they told them

why then?

well, of course, Lola replied
they needed to understand

2

it's just stories for children,
the sister said to the lola
adults over there don't believe
that stuff

oh, they do believe
the lola answered
with a click of her tongue
and shook her head

years later a professor
told her, it's just a myth
adults made up to explain
miscarriages
to "cover up" their grief

but I don't believe any of that
what they said, the sister told her brother
years later, in middle age
over drinks at the Detroit
restaurant that smelled of wet wool coats
and spilt beer and muddy snow
halfway between the cities
they lived in now so far
apart

Henry James told ghost stories
not to children
and not
to explain things

what did he tell them for?

he told them to
take them there

II.

CAREGIVING

some of the parents have begun
to suffer
as you and your friends grow older and more difficult
to lift, like your girlfriend's mother
who slipped a disc and winces
each time she heaves her grown girl
into their van, and uses canes when she believes
her daughter is not looking

your parents have tried to keep it a secret from you
the source of their ailments
whispering within these frail apartment walls
it must be a sad joy
to watch one's son grow into a man
cuteness lost to handsome
features, growing into his own
as they prematurely decay
from all the lifting
of an adult body

the bending over to stretch your spastic legs
so your muscles will not grow slower
than your bones; to wedge your feet into the wheelchair
footplate and bind them down by ripstop
straps; to make sleep possible by alleviating
your pain.
it is one thing to lift a baby or toddler
into your arms
and throw him at the sky laughing
but a man in your arms
must tip you back on your heels

and now, in mid middle age
they sometimes hunch over
and get mistaken for elderly
their crooked necks, backs
arms that burn
so hot
he can barely type

she says every word counts more in poetry
he says, every word burns

ELDERLY LADY

the other day you spotted her
at the park, on her back on the grass
surrounded by two young joggers trying
to help her rise
and was surprised to see it was her
young face still pained
from the caregiver's spasm that knocked
her down

and you wished it was you who had
lifted her

THE ROOSTER

And the yayas always kept a lantern
lit because they believed
children like you can see the dead.

You are a lucky child, your lola tells you
yet another time.
Sit here, beside me, at cards.
In America they used to put lucky children like you
into institutions, away from families

but here we value you, like that time
Tio Salvador took you out on the railroad skit
with your wheelchair strapped
on the plywood platform
to cockfights
within the jungles of plantation Navarro
and his rooster won
pesos that paid for your sweet ice halo halo afterward
at Kawayan market

everything tastes best when bought with
winnings but

best not to think of the razor
claws attached to talons
and the feathers they scattered
as they sought organs within. The villagers believe
dead souls can speak
to the lucky children like you.
One time a yaya who missed her dead
father took you, without telling us
so we thought you had wandered
off lost, and sent out a search party

Salvador so frantic, so mad
we found you in the nipa chapel
the yaya on her knees
before the votive candle
begging you to seek ghost-words of her perished
father.
We heard her crying for mercy
as we hurried you away, clasping our hands
over your ears to protect
you from screaming.

One night, you screamed awake
in the dark
and I asked what was wrong
had you seen the ghost
and you said,
Hindi po, I saw a rooster
its stomach opened, and entrails dangling.

Additional Acknowledgments

Thanks first of all to my family for their patience, inspiration and support of my writing, Gwen, Aidan, Brendan, Tom and Azucena Roley and all the rest. Thanks to Carla Roley for the feedback and images. Much gratitude goes to the following institutions for support during the writing of this project: the National Endowment of the Arts, the Ohio Arts Council, the University of Cambridge, the Virginia Center for the Creative Arts, the Djerassi Foundation, the Ragdale Foundation, and Miami University, especially colleagues whose creative works have inspired me such as Jody Bates, cris cheek, Daisy Hernandez, Margaret Luongo, TaraShea Nesbit, David Schloss, Kay Sloan, Keith Tuma, Cathy Wagner, Peg Faimon and Jon Yamanaka. Thanks to my students who have taught or inspired me and the teachers who have invited me to speak to their students, and department chairs LuMing Mao, Keith Tuma and Madelyn Detloff for support. Thanks to the many Pinoy poets who have shown the way, such as Zach Zamora, Luisa Igloria, Eugene Gloria, Vince Gotera, Cecilia Brainard, and too many others to name.

And of course thanks to all of the staff and editors at Finishing Line Press, including Leah Maines, Kevin Maines, Jacqueline Steelman, and Christen Kincaid.

Brian Ascalon Roley is a writer and professor of Philippine and American descent. He became a National Endowment of the Arts Literature Fellow in 2020.

His books include AMERICAN SON (WW Norton), which was a *New York Times* Editor's Choice and Notable Book of the Year, *Los Angeles Times* Best Book, Kiriyama Pacific Rim Prize Finalist and recipient of the Association for Asian American Studies Prose Book Award in 2003, among other honors. Roley's work has also been featured in the California Council for the Humanities Statewide Reading Campaign of 2004, and has been taught in many classrooms around the country and internationally. His 2016 collection, THE LAST MISTRESS OF JOSE RIZAL, was released by Northwestern University Press.

His work in multiple genres has appeared in many journals and anthologies, including *Mixed: An Anthology of Short Fiction on the Multiracial Experience* (WW Norton), *and Charlie Chan is Dead 2: An Anthology of Contemporary Asian American Fiction* (Penguin), and several best selling anthologies in the Philippines.

Brian has received fellowships and awards from the National Endowment of the Arts, the Ohio Arts Council, the University of Cambridge, Cornell University, the Djerassi Foundation, Ragdale, the VCCA and others. He is Professor of English at Miami University of Ohio. More info at: *www.brianroley.com*.

www.ingramcontent.com/pod-product-compliance
Lightning Source LLC
LaVergne TN
LVHW041551070426
835507LV00011B/1044